SATISFY YOUR SOUL

How to Begin Planting the Seeds of Your Dreams

JOSHUA PEREZ

Visit www.FeelFreetoGrow.com to learn more.

Published by Nooga Media Solutions
P. O. Box 2641
Chattanooga, Tennessee 37409
www.noogamedia.com

Author Cover Photo: Melissa Einarsen

Printed in the United States of America.

First Edition, 2016

ISBN-13: 978-1536910582
ISBN-10: 1536910589

To my kids, who were once only a dream of mine. I'm proud to call each of you my children, and my aim is to do my best to prepare you to live a most satisfying life; one that makes you smile a genuine smile - the kind that comes from the innermost part of you. I can't wait to be a witness of your dreams unfolding.

Contents

Introduction

"My mission in life is not merely to survive, but to thrive; and to do so with some passion, some compassion, some humor, and some style."

-Maya Angelou

Today, my life is more satisfying and fulfilling than ever; I'm healthier physically, mentally, emotionally, and financially than I've ever been before. But at my lowest point, I was very overweight; I was struggling to perform a job that I despised; I was lying to those I loved - but even worse I was lying to myself - about who I really was and what I wanted. Even though I was a Christian pastor, married to a beautiful woman, and we had two beautiful children together, something wasn't right. I longed to be with a man, and frankly, to just be myself, and to no longer have this fat, ugly secret, and the shame that came with it. I was tired of living to please everyone but myself.

The moment everything changed was in 2011 when my mother became very sick and was hospitalized. When I went to see her she began apologizing for several things we had already dealt with in the past. What I realized in that conversation was that she felt like she was at the end of her life, and she had so many regrets for the way she had lived it, and there was nothing at all she could do about it. That experience helped me to realize that I wasn't okay with being 60 or 70 years old, looking back over my life and dying with a long list of regrets.

I decided to start taking better care of myself and living a more healthy, positive, fulfilling life. Since 2011, I've lost over 50 pounds, peacefully ended my heterosexual marriage, and have come out as a proud gay dad who finally loves myself. I have a fulfilling career that excites and challenges me, and frankly, I'm better off financially today than at any other point in my life!

But this life mission doesn't stop with me. Because so many people have invested in me, I'm now compelled to use my life resources to enrich the lives of others. You see, there is a natural law at work; you can't sow a seed, without reaping what you sow. Teachers from my childhood like Ms. Blanchard and Mrs. Ito, seeing the absence of a stable home-life, started investing in me from a young age, not knowing the fruit that would come of it. Senior pastors from my time serving as a youth and young adult pastor taught me about healthy relationships and having the heart of a servant. Countless others have freely and lavishly enriched my life so immensely that the act of now turning to others and empowering them just comes naturally.

My passion is the privilege of personally investing in the lives of others. I've studied relationships and positive psychology for over 15 years. During this time, many people have been drawn to me for my support. Eventually I decided to dedicate my life to helping others like myself overcome life's struggles.

In this book, I'm going to share time-tested tools and strategies I've picked up along my career that will change the direction of your life in positive, meaningful ways. I don't mean to be dramatic here, but the secrets I'm going to share with you can literally alter the course of your life forever; they have mine. Ironically, nothing I'm going to share in this book is *new*. The tools I'm going to offer you are life lessons I've learned from others. And chances are, you've heard some of these ideas, in one form or another, already. Consider me a curator of life hacks that *actually work*. With so many self help books out there today, I wanted to combine in one book those life tools that have really made the biggest difference in my life and in the lives of those I've coached over the years.

Once you see that everything you say and do is a seed planted in the garden of your life - for good or bad - you're then empowered to uproot the weeds that have played leading roles in your nightmares, and replace those painful thorns with seeds that will cause your dreams to burst into the scenes of your everyday life.

Somewhere along the way I started believing I deserve all the good life has to offer. And gradually, but progressively, my life has continued to get better and better. Every experience - the good and the bad - is an opportunity to learn and grow.

It's time for you to go from fear to confidence; from anxiety to peace; and from inaction to success! You deserve all the good life has to offer, too. But "to whom much was given, of him much will be required". The good life doesn't just fall into place. You not only need dreams for tomorrow, but consistent action today. Tomorrow's reality is created by the choices and actions you take (or don't take) today.

If you begin to live the ideas I am going to share with you, day by day you'll begin to see the good life more and more, till one day you'll look around and smile, realizing your dreams are no longer something you're running after, but you're actually living them.

The purpose of me writing this first book is to put a resource in your hands that will spark growth in your life; to help you cultivate healthy relationships; to help enlighten your mind, that you'll be able to reconcile areas of confusion and see that you truly do reap what you sow, so that in turn you'll be inspired to sow what you want to grow. I desire to strengthen your strengths, mend and heal your weak spots, and empower you to thrive in the garden of life. I not only want to inspire you to dream bigger, but I want to enable you to start taking bigger steps. It's time to revive your soul; your night is over, and the sun is rising on your life!

Dream blockers can be found in three primary relationships:

1. the relationship you have with yourself
2. the relationship you have with others
3. the relationship you have with your dreams

In the pages that follow I'll uncover the weeds that have blocked my own dreams from coming true, and the powerful strategies that helped me uproot those weeds, and begin to truly live the life of my dreams.

Part 1: The Relationship with Yourself

CHAPTER 1
Self-Care

"Self-care is not selfish. You cannot serve from an empty vessel."

-Eleanor Brown

It was April 27, 2011, a day that started like any other Wednesday for me: a half hour drive to downtown Chattanooga to begin my day of work. Shortly after arriving though, it became clear this wasn't going to be a typical Wednesday. Reports of tornadic activity were all over the news and social media. Thanks to the clear warnings from local forecasters, I decided to go home to be with my family, and ride out the storms together. What followed for us was 15 hours of panic, followed by relief. We alternated between watching weather reports, and staring at the sky. By day's end, the 2011 Super Outbreak became the largest, costliest, and one of the deadliest tornado outbreaks ever recorded. In total, 348 people lost their lives; it was a terrible day.

Late that night, after learning that members of the church I was serving had lost family members, I started to consider how I could help best. I reached out to ministry friend Sean Malone, founder of Crisis Response International (CRI), a non-profit organization that trains and mobilizes volunteers to respond to disaster and crisis situations around the world. He and his team were quickly en-route from Missouri with volunteers and equipment to help us respond to the worst disaster to hit our town.

For nearly two weeks I helped lead a response to serve those in need. I was thankful my family and our home weren't harmed by the storms, and I felt it was my responsibility as a leader to serve. I spent 16 to 20 hour days coordinating logistics, rallying volunteers, soliciting donations, and much more. That month I sent and received over 10,000 text messages, when before that my plan only allowed a mere 800. My personal web development company was essentially put on hold.

Several times during the outreach, Sean would pull me aside and remind me of the importance of *taking care of myself*: sleeping, eating, praying, meeting the needs of my own family. He even offered practical tips on how to take care of my needs in the middle of responding to such devastation. This was the first time the idea of self-care had really been introduced to me in such a practical, yet critical way. A couple months later I attended one of CRI's training events near D.C. and was again reminded time and again of how critically important it is to *care for ourselves first*, if we want to be effective at caring for others. If you've ever flown, you know as soon as you board you'll be reminded that, in the event of an emergency, you should place your own oxygen mask on before attempting to help others.

The area of self-care is the most important place to focus if you want to see your dreams come true. The relationship you have with yourself really is the foundation of living a happy life; it's the soil in which everything else is planted. To have your dreams come true, you need to be *ready* for them. You need to have a mind that *perceives* that your dreams are coming true. You need an active, healthy body that has the energy to live your dreams. So to begin, I'm going to share the foundational keys of healthy living.

Healthy Living

In today's world, everywhere you turn there is new information about what is bad for you. I have no interest in sharing fads or trends with you, so don't worry. As I said in the introduction, I am going to share time-tested tools and strategies I've picked up along my career that will change the direction of your life in positive, meaningful ways, not gimmicks or trendy fads. That said, some of the ideas may seem elementary - because they are. The problem is, as basic as they are, they are grossly ignored in our culture, and we are suffering the consequences. Love yourself by applying these foundational truths consistently, and I assure you - you will reap the rewards!

The fundamental keys to living a healthy life are simple: sleep deep, nourish your body, and exercise today.

Sleep Deep

In *The Sleep Revolution*, Arianna Huffington makes the case that lack of sufficient sleep compromises our health and our decision-making and undermines our work lives, our personal lives, and even our sex lives. Countless studies show the effect both the quality and quantity of sleep have on our concentration and focus, emotions, and even critically important things like our immune system and cell growth. We need sleep to rejuvenate the mind and spirit as much as the physical body. As we sleep, we release our fears and frustrations and give in to peaceful slumber.

Depending on your age and activity level, experts recommend between 7 and 9 hours of quality sleep each night. Simply determine what time you need to wake up each day, subtract the needed hours of sleep, subtract another 30 minutes and make this your bedtime. If you have a partner you sleep with, or if you have plans on certain evenings, make others aware of your bedtime.

Ideas for improving the quality of your sleep are to keep your bedroom dark, quiet, and cool, no electronic devices starting 30 minutes before bedtime (including TV and your phone), don't allow pets or children to sleep in bed with you, and invest in comfort - everything from your pj's to your mattress, sheets, and pillows should be pleasing and comfortable to you.

Nourish Your Body

As I shared in the introduction, I used to be quite heavy. I began to make progress when I began to change my mind about how I thought of myself in relation to food and exercise. Two mantras I said to myself then (and still do to this day) are:

1. Food is fuel, not fun.
2. There is an athlete inside of everyone.

Somewhere between adolescence and adulthood I began thinking of food as merely pleasure. Even my kids knew my favorite hobby was Mayfield's Moose Tracks ice cream. When grocery shopping or preparing a meal, my focus was almost completely on what would *taste* good.

At 232 pounds, I finally realized I needed to make changes. I began paying attention to calories, carbs, etc. I had apps that would track my consumption. A shift took place in my mind from seeing food as something to bring me happiness, to seeing food as fuel to energize me and keep me going through my day.

This isn't a diet book, and I'm not going to lay out meal plans or calorie intake recommendations. There are plenty of resources available free of charge online for those who need them. My charge to you is to begin focusing on nourishment for your body. You aren't finished on earth yet. You have several years ahead of you, and you need a reliable vehicle - your body - to use. So, meal-prep if you have to. Go on a diet if you need to lose weight. But focus on nourishing the cells of your body. Give yourself the nutrients you need. Eat foods that make your mind and body *feel* good. Lastly, be sure to hydrate your body by drinking the right amount of water.

Exercise Today

There truly is no better time to exercise than today. Whether you like to walk your dog each evening after work, or you're into extreme CrossFit routines, find what you enjoy, then do it...today! Plan for it, and make it a priority. As with nourishing your body, my intention is not to lay out workout regiments or to recommend a certain type of exercise even; what's important is that you actually do something physical. Today. (No, really...go.)

DREAM BLOCKERS: *Lack of quality sleep, failing to nourish your body with good foods and adequate water, not having a plan for exercise*

SEEDS TO YOUR DREAMS: *Sleep deep, nourish your body with fresh foods and sufficient water consumption, be intentional about exercising in some way every day*

CHAPTER 2

Self-Love

"Dare to love yourself as if you were a rainbow with gold at both ends."

-Aberjhani

Entire books have been written on this topic alone, and many more still need to be written. The lack of self-love is without question the biggest culprit to both relationship and health problems. Author Louise Hay is a beautiful soul who has had a tremendous impact on my life, and countless others. Louise says, "After years of individual counseling with clients and conducting hundreds of workshops and intensive training programs across the country and around the world, I found that there is only one thing that heals every problem, and that is: to know how to love yourself." Addressing this one issue would decrease the divorce rate, the suicide rate, decrease the number of prescriptions written, and so many other problems facing our world.

Most adults pridefully assert that they love themselves without actually exploring the topic and dealing with the issue. The way they live their lives is plenty evidence to the contrary - that they barely know themselves, much less love and cherish and have positive regard for themselves. There is no way for me to give this topic the time it deserves in this chapter, but I want to share a few really good places to get you started.

Louise Hay defines self-love as having a deep appreciation for who we are. Today, right where you are, in the middle of all your mess, having a deep appreciation and full acceptance of all of you. Nothing soothes the soul like being able to look yourself in the eyes, being more intimately aware of all your flaws than anyone, and still being able to smile and say, "I really love you", knowing that it's true.

Mirror Work

I want to introduce you to a powerful healing practice that has changed so many lives. Without exception, this is a practice I teach every one of my coaching clients, and without fail I have seen its healing effect in all of their lives, and also in my own life. Louise Hay's exercise she calls "Mirror Work" is the act of building a healthy, loving relationship with the most important person in your life - you. In this exercise, you affirm your love for yourself. It goes like this...

Go to a mirror, and take a deep breath. Now look yourself in the eyes and focus. Then say your name, followed by "I love you. I really, really love you. I really love you, today." For some, this may provoke positive emotions, but for many it may also bring painful or negative emotions to the surface; and that is okay. Your emotions need to be felt, whatever they are. If saying "I love you" is too much for you at first, begin the first week or so by saying your name, followed by "I am willing to learn to love you (or like you) today." As you do this exercise multiple times a day, you may notice that proof of what you're saying comes to mind. For example, often times when I am doing my Mirror Work, positive changes I've made recently in my life come to mind that affirm in me that I do indeed really love me. Another benefit of the exercise that I really enjoy is new ways of loving yourself will come to your mind; things you realize that, in order to demonstrate you love yourself, you should stop doing, or start doing, or maybe do more or less of.

Treat Yourself

Another practical way to love yourself is by treating yourself. How to do this will look different to different people, but let me share how it looks to me:

I have a "me night". The first thing I do is turn off my phone. Then I turn on my favorite spa music playlist and pour a glass of wine. Next I apply a facemask, and I sit. Listening to the soothing music, sipping my soothing wine, I sit and relax. After the facemask has worked it's magic, I take an extra long, extra hot shower and exfoliate my skin. If I feel like it, I'll even do a little mani pedi action. Afterwards, I moisturize every inch of my body, including my hair. Then I light a eucalyptus candle, and change the music to a guided meditation that peaks my interest. At this point I usually fall asleep, earlier than my normal bedtime, and catch up on some much needed deep sleep.

The way you feel "treated" is probably different than mine, but the point is to pamper yourself - doing those things that often don't make the cut on our daily to-do lists.

Forward Thinking

Another way to love yourself is to act on the deep needs of your soul, rather than simply medicating yourself with lesser short-term pleasures.

Shortly after my divorce, I found myself free to do as I pleased, no longer being accountable to a life partner. I began drinking alcohol several nights a week, which eased my mind from having to deal with the more painful realities of life for a short time. As you can imagine, this also cost me a great deal. Physically speaking, it cost me sleep and energy and focus. Financially, it cost me missed opportunities, lost clients, late fees, interest, etc.

Thankfully, I eventually became more self aware, and I saw how this new habit was costing me so much. Not only was I not making progress toward my life goals, in most areas I felt I was actually sliding backwards. I revisited the goals and action plans I had written for myself (I will be sharing a

Focused Life Plan in chapter 9 of this book), revising them as needed, and I got to work. I found my healthy balance. When you turn away from something that feels good and exciting in the moment to focus on what you need to feel alive, balanced, and moving forward towards your dreams, you're actually demonstrating that you love yourself. And you're showing the universe that you fully intend to attract your dreams into your reality. Turn away from self-defeating behaviors, commitments, and relationships that steal your most valuable life resources of time, focus, and energy, and turn towards that future that you daydream about.

DREAM BLOCKERS: *Lack of a quality, loving relationship with yourself, failing to meet your own needs, settling for lesser momentary pleasures*

__SEEDS TO YOUR DREAMS:__ Mirror Work, developing a real relationship with yourself, treating yourself and ensuring all your own needs are met, sacrificing some lesser pleasures for the greater pleasure of living your dreams

CHAPTER 3
Self-Confidence

"The world will see you the way you see you, and treat you the way you treat yourself."

-Beyoncé

Imagine Beyoncé as a young, shy child in elementary school. As she is waiting for her parents to pick her up from dance class, she overhears her dance instructor humming a song to herself. "I know this song", she thinks to herself. As student of dance, I imagine she was probably tapping her foot. But it's what Beyoncé chose to do next that has turned out to be a defining moment in her life. She sang. Her instructor says she hit magical notes, and encouraged her to sing it again.

But what if this story had gone differently. What if Beyoncé allowed her shyness to keep her quiet in that moment? Beyoncé credits that moment as the first time someone encouraged her singing. When her parents arrived, the instructor told them that she could sing really well. After that, her parents started signing her up for singing competitions and the rest is history.

Many people refuse to sing in front of others, reserving it only for alone time in the car or in the shower. If she had allowed the voices of self-doubt to keep her quiet, she would have never sold over 160 million records, and all those shiny Grammy awards would not have been hers for the taking.

Our natural tendency is to minimize our abilities and to magnify the perceived abilities of others. This isn't reality though. You need to know you are braver than you believe, stronger than you seem, smarter than you think, and twice as capable as you have ever imagined.

Unfuckwithable Confidence

I like to call this mindset Unfuckwithable Confidence: the constant awareness of what an amazing badass you are, regardless of what others say or do or think about you. Because, as I'll discuss later in this book, what others say and do has much more to do with them and what's going on inside them than it does you. I can't stress enough how important it is to be aware of how badass you really are. Start telling yourself what you love about yourself. Remember even your biggest fears don't actually exist. They aren't reality. They are merely fears. Thoughts. Don't let fear chart the course of your life, or steal another chapter of your book. As you develop in the areas of self-love, self-care, and self-confidence, you will be in a healthier, more balanced position to begin relating to others in a way that *attracts your dreams into your life.*

Before you move on to part 2 of this book, *The Relationship with Others*, consider taking some time to evaluate your relationship with yourself. It can't be emphasized enough how critical it is that your relationship with yourself is healthy. It is the foundation of every other relationship you have, especially romantic or love relationships. You do a disservice to yourself and the person you date when you enter a relationship with another person before developing a healthy relationship with you first.

Everyone needs love, but many people are also "needy" for love. Being needy for love is caused by missing the love and approval that should come from yourself. When this is missing, many people turn to others to fill the void only they can fill. And this neediness sabotages many relationships. Do yourself a favor and take the time to cultivate a genuine love for yourself. Learn to enjoy your own company. Take inventory (literally make a list) of the things about yourself that you like, and the things about yourself that you're proud of. Another wonderful benefit to developing a healthier relationship with yourself is, you'll notice you will begin to attract healthier people to you as well, which makes for happier, more fulfilling relationships.

DREAM BLOCKERS: *Minimizing your abilities, doubting yourself and your dreams, allowing the fear of what others thing to hold you back from your dreams*

SEEDS TO YOUR DREAMS: *Giving yourself permission to be brave, strong, smart, and capable, unfuckwithable confidence, not making other people's opinions any of your business*

Part 2: The Relationship with Others

CHAPTER 4
Caring For Others

"The entire fabric of our society...relies on the positive beliefs we have about each other."

-Marc Chernoff

Ironically, the prerequisite to building healthy relationships is being comfortable when you're all by yourself. Once you're able to stand in front of a mirror, look yourself in the eyes, and say "I love you" and know deep inside that it's true, you can then begin to evaluate your relationships with others, including your friends, coworkers, family, children, spouses, and even adversaries.

Ask any life coach, counselor, psychologist, or pastor and I'm sure they will tell you the topic of relationships is something everyone seems to seek help with. In fact, 100% of my clients have asked for help with their relationships with others.

I heard a story once of a psychologist who was asked to provide counseling to a group of refugees who had experienced all kinds of horrific experiences. What do you suppose these hurting people wanted to talk to her about? Their relationships.

Relationships are the most valuable part of our lives. Unfortunately, they are also the part of our lives that require the most work. However, the right relationships are worth the effort. To help you determine what relationships to continue investing in, and which ones may need to be pruned to one degree or another, consider the following foundational elements of a healthy relationship:

Trust

Ask yourself questions like: "Can I trust this person?" and "Do others trust this person?"...if the answer to any of these is no, be sure you have valid, factual reasons why you feel you can't trust them. You don't want to make the mistake of deciding you can't trust someone simply based on assumptions you've made that you don't know to be factual. However, if you determine this person can't be trusted, you should consider either distancing yourself a little (at least until they demonstrate their trustworthiness over time), or even ending the relationship, depending on the circumstances.

Respect

Signs that you are respected in a relationship are:
- they listen to your thoughts and ideas
- they recognize and admire your good qualities
- they honor your boundaries
- when disagreements happen - and they will - they "fight fairly"

If you aren't being respected, it may be time to have a conversation with the other person. Sometimes we just get comfortable in our relationships; we are all human. If your friend or family member cares about you, they will listen to your concerns, and be willing to make appropriate changes to how they relate to you. If not, it may be time to consider what role this relationship will have in your future.

Enrichment

One of the most wonderful elements to a relationship can be the enrichment to our lives someone can bring. In the fall of 2012, in the middle of my divorce, I met the most amazing friend I've ever had, Valerie. I was obviously an emotional roller coaster at that time in my life, mostly due to the pain of going from a lifestyle of seeing my children every day of their lives, to having shared custody of them.

Valerie was more than a friend; she was my counselor, my sounding board, my encourager, my balance, the one who reminded me of all I had to look forward to in life, the one who believed in me on some of the ugliest days of my life, when I didn't even believe in myself, or think anyone else could.

As time healed the pain of my divorce, she enriched my life by pushing me to try new experiences, meet new people, travel to new places, begin new adventures, and yes, try new wines.

Valerie is a Scorpio like me; in fact, she and I are so much alike, there have been countless times we've *accurately* read each other's mind. She knows me better than anyone else. But because we are so much alike, we tend to butt heads from time to time. After arguments with her, I've often joked that if only I were straight, or *she* were a *he*, we could just give up and marry one another. She and I have had dozens of multi-hour long phone calls, and not one of them was a burden. On the contrary, I've found more clarity and understanding in our conversations than I ever could have alone.

Relationships, in their highest form, will be *mutually enriching*. In a perfect scenario, each person in a relationship will feel that the other adds value to his or her life in a meaningful way. Due to the ebbs and flows of life, sometimes one of you will be more the giver, where the other will be more the taker. In some relationships, like a parent/child relationship, teacher/student relationship, or a mentoring or coaching relationship, the playing field isn't level and one will naturally bring more to the relationship than the other. Some things to consider when evaluating whether a particular relationship is enriching your life are:

- Are they committed to excellence?
- Do we bring out the best in each other?
- Does this relationship refresh me or drain me?

Once you're able to determine what relationships deserve your effort, you can begin to invest your most valuable life resources (time, energy, and money) into growing them. After all, healthy relationships are an important key to living your dreams. *Healthy relationships will be a support system to your dreams.* Unhealthy relationships will be violently destructive to your dreams.

I vaguely remember once, when I was a young boy, trying to use a tiller in the garden. I wasn't very strong, and I had no experience using the equipment. Needless to say, I didn't accomplish much more than a mess.

Think of healthy relationships as the fertilizer of your dreams. They support and enhance "the good life" in every way. On the other hand, think of unhealthy relationships as an eight year old little boy running an out of control tiller through your dreams...you get the picture.

Now that you've learned how to determine what relationships will support your dreams, I am going to share a few tools that will nurture those relationships.

The Mountaintop of Life

My favorite place to escape alone to think or pray is the mountains. In fact, my office sits at the bottom of Lookout Mountain in Chattanooga, Tennessee. Several times a week I drive up the mountain to a breath-taking overlook called Sunset Rock. This beautiful hideaway overlooks the winding Tennessee River, which cuts through Chattanooga, as well as Interstate 75. Often when I see the tiny cars zooming by from such a height, I wonder where the driver is headed, or who they may be. This bird's eye view really has a way of altering my perspective.

With that scene in mind, imagine with me for a moment that you've come to the last few days of your life, and this wise, experienced, gray-headed you is standing on the mountaintop of life, and you're looking down over your life. You see this much younger, less experienced you facing difficult times, and stumbling, but getting back up and pushing forward through all the ups and downs of life. You see the mistakes you made due to lack of knowledge, the things you would have done differently if your beliefs were then what they are now, and the chances you didn't take due to pain you were still holding on to.

From this perspective, don't you think you would be a little more understanding, accepting, and forgiving of yourself? Don't you think you were doing your best with the circumstances you were facing?

Now, let's apply this same perspective to the relationships you have with others. Wouldn't this more seasoned you trust that they, too, are doing their best? And if they are doing their best, what really needs to be forgiven? Not being perfect?

The truth is, as entertaining as Beyoncé's song may be, no one is "Flawless". We all have strengths and weaknesses. So above all, learn the power of acceptance. Accepting "what is" is the path to peace and happiness. When you remove the obstacles we call expectations from a relationship, there is suddenly room to dance together freely. There is no feeling like knowing someone knowing *all* of you, the good, bad, and the ugly, and loves you just the same.

Boundaries

Another relationship tool that will help you have healthy, long-term relationships is having healthy boundaries. According to *Merriam Webster Dictionary* a boundary is "a point or limit that indicates where two things become different". It is where I stop and you begin. When boundaries are crossed, one or both people in a relationship are taken advantage of, or are regularly made to feel uncomfortable, which puts stress on the relationship. Codependency can also become an issue between you.

To set healthy boundaries, ask yourself what you can accept and tolerate, and what makes you unhappy or uncomfortable in a relationship. When you have healthy boundaries in a relationship, you are able to:

- say no without feeling guilt or shame
- say yes because you want to say yes
- ask for what you need
- take care of your needs without feeling guilt or shame
- honor your own beliefs and values with your choices and actions
- feel safe, even during disagreements
- feel equal in the relationship
- expect each person to be responsible for their own happiness

No Assumptions Allowed

If I were to ask you what the first step in beginning a relationship with someone was, you would likely include "getting to know someone" in your response, right? When we first meet someone, our mind creates a character, which we believe this person to be. If our first impression of this person is positive, we will create in our mind a whole list of characteristics about this person we suspect to be true; honest, kind, someone we could see being friends with. If the first impression is negative, however, the list of characteristics we begin to believe to be true of them, even in a matter of a few minutes, would include dishonest, selfish, untrustworthy, and we would begin to build boundaries or walls to ensure we don't get hurt or taken advantage of by this person.

As time passes we begin to get to know this person. We learn the true characteristics of who this person is. We observe their choices and actions. We gather facts. The assumptions we made when we first encountered this person often turn out to be incorrect. Have you ever known of a person, maybe someone at work or at school, who you had a less than favorable opinion of before getting to know them, only to spend time with them and learn they aren't so bad? I've had this experience multiple times in my life; some people I didn't have a good first impression of have turned out to be really good friends.

Unfortunately, this habit of making assumptions takes place daily in most people's lives. They assume they know what another person is thinking, or their motivation for doing something, when they really have no clue. They assume that others also have this same gift of mind reading and are fully aware of their needs and expectations, even though they've never been communicated.

In the life-transforming book *The Four Agreements*, don Miguel Ruiz explains that the problem with making assumptions is that we believe they are true. Then we base our decisions and our interactions with others on these false-truths too. Next, we take this error a step further by taking what we believe to be happening *personally*. What others say and do to you and about you actually has nothing to do with you. The truth is, what others say and do has to do with what is going on inside their own mind and emotions. If someone says something to others about you that isn't true, does that make it true? Of course not. What they said about you has to do with what's going on inside their mind and emotions at that moment. It's not really true, and it's not your business to be worried about what's going inside their mind. So, remember: don't take things others say and do personally, and don't make assumptions; say what you need to say, and ask the questions you need to ask to find understanding in a situation. Don't try to read other people's mind, and don't expect others to be able to read your mind either. This will only create needless relationship drama.

DREAM BLOCKERS: *Holding on to relationships that lack trust, respect, and enrichment, not accepting the humanness of others,* *lacking healthy relationship boundaries, trying to mind-read and taking things personally*

SEEDS TO YOUR DREAMS: *Develop trust, respect and mutual enrichment in your relationships, allow those in your life to still be human, have and practice healthy boundaries in all your relationships, ask questions and tell others what they need to know, and don't take what others do or don't do personally*

CHAPTER 5
Loving Others

"The most important ingredient in a comfortable, intimate, long term relationship...is mutual acceptance."

-Pat Mellody

The primary purpose of love relationships is to allow two people to be connected to each other through intimacy in a way that provides both people with support, easing the burdens of life, and enhancing the enjoyment of living. I believe strongly that life is meant to be *shared*. To me, relationships are the most valuable part of life. In this chapter I am going to share with you some relationship lessons I've learned personally that, if applied to your own life, will strengthen your own relationships. My focus will be on love relationships between dating or married couples, but really these ideas can be helpful in all relationships.

My purpose for writing this book is to curate the ideas and life lessons I've been fortunate to receive that have made the biggest difference, and share them with others, because I believe in them! I'm not aiming to make a name for myself. This book isn't about me; it's about improving the lives of others with tools that work. That said, however, I would like to briefly share some of my own story related to love relationships.

In 2012, shortly after my divorce, I did what many newly single divorcees do: I started meeting new people. I went on dates, had one night stands, dating app profiles, etc. I met a lot of great people, some interesting characters, and made some friends. Truth be told, I wasn't ready for a serious relationship, but I didn't really realize that at the time. Hindsight is always 20/20, right? Anyway, a few years in, and a couple serious relationships squandered, I finally realized I had some work to do on my relationship with myself before I would be truly ready to have a healthy, long-term relationship with anyone else. So as another relationship came to an end, I decided not to allow myself to enter another relationship for a while. I started seeing a coach to guide me through addressing some of the issues I felt I needed help with. During this process of self-discovery and growth, I learned so much! While single, with plenty of free time not being occupied by a boyfriend, I had a chance to get to know myself more. I also had a chance to evaluate some of the expectations I used to have in relationships. Some of them, I realized, were just silly. Some of them needed a little tweaking, and some of them I kept. Through this process I also adopted some new ways of looking at relationships.

In all my past relationships, I never felt my expectations were being met. I was constantly disappointed, and always wanted to discuss things I felt needed to improve in the relationship. What I didn't realize at the time was, I was trying to fix something in the relationship with the person I was dating, when the real issue was in the relationship with myself. There was a void inside me, and I was expecting the person I was dating to fill what only I could fill.

Many people refer to their mate as their "other half" and tell others that their mate "completes" them. In movies, this always sounds *so* romantic and dreamy, but in reality it's descriptive of an unhealthy relationship. To search for someone to complete you insinuates that you aren't whole by yourself. Perhaps this is one reason so many relationships tend to fall apart. People who haven't even started to build a healthy, fulfilling relationship with themselves are venturing out into the dating world, expecting someone else to give them what only they can give themselves.

As discussed in part one of this book, the relationship you have with yourself is the foundation of every other relationship in your life. If you lack a healthy, loving, fulfilling relationship with yourself, when you enter a relationship with someone else you will eventually place expectations on them that are really your responsibility to meet. Before you know it, you'll begin feeling that your partner isn't "meeting your needs" in the relationship, when really the issue is that you haven't learned to meet your own needs yet. Then you will likely begin giving disproportionate amounts of time and attention to the other person in the relationship; some of which belongs to you. You will continue to have this feeling of your needs not being met, meanwhile in your mind you begin to struggle with feelings of disappointment and betrayal by your significant other. You won't understand why, if they love you, they aren't meeting your unrealistic expectations. The stress and tone of the relationship will change due to the negative pressure you're putting on the relationship until you will begin to sense that the other person is now distancing and detaching themselves somewhat from you and the relationship.

The Three Gets

12 step programs teach a very healthy relationship strategy called "The Three Gets" which really helps one take a step back, out of the downward spiral I just described. The Three Gets are:

1. **Get off your partner's back.** Don't constantly look for what they are or are not doing so that you can evaluate it. Instead, regard what they do or don't do as none of your business. Merely *notice* their actions, so you can observe who they truly are.

2. **Get out of your partner's way.** Don't interfere with their life by trying to give "helpful advice" or by making critical

statements of them. Again, consider this none of your business.

3. **Get on with your life.** Instead of allowing your partner's life to consume yours, live your own life! Get to know yourself and your dreams. Learn to love yourself. Learn to meet your own needs. I assure you, you will be so much happier if you do.

In healthy relationships, you are able to nurture others in a way that promotes their emotional and spiritual growth and promotes their taking responsibility for themselves, thereby increasing their self-esteem. The grand purpose of life is to give you a platform, a banquet table if you will, for giving and receiving love.

I was pleasantly surprised to find that what I first thought was an ending, turned out to be the beginning of a time of personal growth. Today, I'm single and very happy. Because I believe life is meant to be shared, I would be thankful if my mate entered my life soon. But I also know myself well enough to know that not just anyone will do. It's going to take a very special person to fill that position. In the meantime, I've found a refreshing contentment with spending time alone, and working towards my dreams. In fact, it's given me the time I needed to write this book, a dream of mine for many years.

Acceptance

One last point I'll leave you with regarding loving others: as you slowly navigate the path of love relationships, remember that you are only human, and so is the other person. With balance, it's certainly good to have certain standards in a relationship. After all, you are the one that knows best what type of relationship you desire. Every human, however, has flaws and imperfections. Some of those flaws are fixable, if the person wants to fix them. However, there are some "issues" that we die with. They don't go away, and may not even get better. And a person will only change when they want to. Therefore, date someone who has flaws you can live with, or even appreciate. I believe the most accurate metric for your love of someone is how you relate to their flaws. If you're able to accept them, or even master the art of adoring their shortcomings, and they can learn to do the same, that is a picture of true intimacy.

That said, it's also important to accept that not every couple is meant to be a couple. And that's okay! Although not all relationships will last, don't miss the value of growing from those that don't. Instead of being bitter because things didn't go as planned, celebrate your past, embrace your present reality, and allow belief in your dreams to grow by faith!

DREAM BLOCKERS: *Bouncing from relationship to relationship without taking a break to learn and grow, constantly critiquing those you're in relationship with, living through your* *partner's life instead of your own, not accepting who your partner is, flaws and all*

SEEDS TO YOUR DREAMS: *Take time between seasons to learn and grow, get off your partner's back, out of their way, and live your own life, learn to love even the flaws your partner has, and if you can't accept who your partner is, consider moving on*

CHAPTER 6

Serving Others

"Do what you have to do until you can do what you want to do."

-Oprah Winfrey

It was an abnormally long, hot summer in the humid state of Tennessee one July, and I found myself doing the most unpleasant of jobs. I was working for a company that produced goods for a major retailer in the United States, and a very large, annual order was late being shipped. Now, my position was not normally based in the hot manufacturing plant that I was working in that day. It was in the climate-controlled corporate office on the other side of town. I was responsible for managing the daily reporting and analysis of our largest account. I loved my job! Not only did I enjoy the challenge of my responsibilities, I was offered this job at a time when I was very desperate for work. I had been unemployed, due to no fault of my own, for 7 months that year, so this job was a *lifesaver*.

I wasn't always so positive about the job though. An employment agency hired by the company somehow stumbled upon an outdated copy of my resume online and reached out to me about the position. The woman from the employment agency who called me about the position wasn't very knowledgeable or professional, and her description of the position was even less appealing. She said the position would be in a manufacturing facility that would often be hot in the summer and cold in the winter, and that the position would entail lots of mundane repetition (something I despise). However, because I was so desperate for work, I agreed to interview for the position, at least for a source of income until I could find something better.

Fortunately, when I met with the president of the company and he reviewed my experience and skills, he thought of another position that I was a better fit for (and one that I was much more interested in).

Fast-forward a couple years later, to where I started this story: doing a most unpleasant job. The workers in the plant had been working long overtime in the heat for weeks, and the president decided to give them the day off, and let the corporate staff come work in the plant that day. Even though I had a very comfortable office on the other side of town, my boss (the president of the company) was doing the same thing I was doing, so I couldn't really complain. I was literally dripping sweat as I loaded more than half a tractor-trailer full of boxes by hand.

An hour or so into this sauna experience, I started complaining in my mind. "This isn't what I was hired to do", I thought. Then I quickly remembered that the president of the company, whose father founded the company, was spending the day doing the same kind of work. I knew that I needed to change my attitude, so I started saying my positive affirmations. As I did this, though, I thought of an even deeper meaning to the work I was doing that day.

Sowing Into My Dreams

I decided to inform the universe that the work I was doing that day - filling a trailer with boxes full of another man's product - was a seed I was sowing for my future. I began to envision the hundreds of boxes I was stacking as my own product. Future books that I would write would be boxed and shipped to retailers around the world! I began to imagine someone else, dripping sweat, loading a trailer full of my products one day. Suddenly, this work became worth it to me. In fact, I was excited to see just how much work I could get done, and found myself pushing my physical limits.

The best part of that story is that I had just started writing this book as that story unfolded in my life. The book you are holding in your hands is evidence that you do indeed reap what you sow.

As you begin to experience more and more growth in the relationships with yourself and others, you will begin to find yourself in a place where you are ready and capable of living your dreams. Most people don't find themselves immediately living all of their dreams all on the same day though. Living your dreams is a progressive work, something that builds upon itself, just like many streams and creeks fill a rushing river. Therefore, as you're growing in this progressive experience, *always remember* that you will see the repercussions of your choices and actions, good or bad. So, choose to love what you do, until you can do what you love. Even if that means tricking your mind as I did in the story above. You may not have the job of your dreams today, but that doesn't mean you can't enjoy the journey. Having a positive attitude and working hard will always be rewarded, even if you can't connect the dots.

Work/Life Balance

That also means you need to maintain balance in your life, even while working hard towards your dreams. Don't allow boundaries to be consistently crossed that cause you to *get more done* at the cost of your relationship with yourself or those you love most. Give yourself permission to say no sometimes. A good work-life balance will allow you to accomplish great things, while still having a fulfilling, refreshing personal life. It's not either/or, it's both/and.

I love lists. My phone has hundreds of them. As I write this, my phone has, to name only a few, a list of:

- Things I need from the store
- A "big purchase" wish list
- An idea list for this book
- A to-do list for my web development company
- A list of movies I want to see
- A list of things I need to do around my house
- A bucket list

Focus

The last list I am going to tell you about has been the object of many jokes from my friends. And I'm at peace with it...because it has worked for me! Every hour on the hour from 8 AM - 8 PM, my phone has an alert called "FOCUS" that reminds me to FOCUS! By now I know what that means, but in case I ever forget, I have a list of reminders inside that alert. These are things that are really important for me to remember on a daily basis. The list gets revised about once a year or so, but it goes something like this:

1. Think positively.
2. Eat healthy.
3. Exercise today.
4. Worry less.
5. Laugh more.
6. Work hard.
7. Have fun.
8. Sleep deep.

The magic of this annoying hourly reminder is it keeps me focused on what really brings quality to my life. And an added benefit regarding work is it also helps me get back on track if my attention has wandered, as it often does. (SQUIRREL!)

Whatever your life's work is - whether you serve many, or many serve you - do your life's work well.

DREAM BLOCKERS: *Despising the good things already in your life, being a "yes man", forgetting about your dreams and goals*

SEEDS TO YOUR DREAMS: *Value and be thankful for the good things in your life today, learn when to say no for the sake of balance, put reminders of your dreams throughout your days, weeks, months, and years*

Part 3: The Relationship with Your Dreams

CHAPTER 7

Seeing Your Dreams

"You'll always tend to see whatever it is you're looking for."

-Michael Neill

Now that we are turning our attention to the relationship you have with your dreams, I want to share an experience in my life that has proved to be a defining moment in my career. The lesson I learned from this experience has altered the course of my career, and my life as a whole.

As you read the final part of this book, I implore you to proceed with your imagination *activated*. Be open to new ideas, new possibilities, and a higher level of *belief*. If you read the next 3 chapters with a mindset of skepticism or doubt, you will be wasting your time. Disbelief has no productive agent, no creative flow, and no life-giving force. Imagination combined with belief, however, are a magical combination that can be likened to Miracle-Gro for your dreams. When the thoughts you imagine about your dreams are combined with the feeling of *belief* or certainty, this powerful combination begins to influence your thoughts and actions in a way that rapidly attracts your dreams into your life like a magnet.

Though other experiences in my life tried to teach me this lesson, the moment it "stuck" for me was a few years ago when I was living in Florida for a season. I was working for a professional association in the state capital at the time, but I had started looking for a position closer to home so I could move back to Tennessee and be closer to my children. Due to health concerns, the director of the association resigned, and the board approached me to help them operate the association in the interim. I was really ready to leave, and had actually already informed them of my intentions. I had several conversations with my best friend as I was trying to decide whether to stay or not, which changed the way I saw the situation. I went from seeing this as an inconvenience to a grand opportunity for me. I started looking at the situation as an opportunity to advance my career. I *saw myself* as worth more than I was currently receiving. In the process, I started *seeing myself* as worthy of all the good life has to offer, and gradually, but progressively, my life has continued to get better and better.

For the first time in my life, I asked for a promotion and a raise. In exchange for staying to help them during the transition, I asked for a 50% raise, and that I be considered for the position of executive director. I got a significant raise, though not equal to 50%, and I wasn't offered the position of executive director, but I did assume the responsibilities until someone else was hired, which gave me an incredibly valuable experience that I was able to add to my resume. Perhaps the biggest reward I received from this experience, though, was the lessons I learned. I came to a greater understanding of two things:

1. the impact of how we view ourselves and our experiences
2. the reward of asking for what we want or need

You're The Driver

When I first learned that the executive director went on a leave of absence due to health concerns, I thought to myself "Great. Perfect timing. Just as I was trying to leave myself." I was looking at the situation as a problem. I saw the timing as inconvenient for me. I viewed it as a setback to my plans. Once I changed how I looked at the situation, however, and began viewing this as an opportunity to step-up instead of as a setback, everything changed. The universe began to support my dreams. I was given favor with the board, and favor with the employees. I received the largest raise I had ever received at that point in my career, and the experience I gained has impacted my ability to receive better job offers and higher pay. These days, when anything comes my way that resembles a *problem*, I whisper to myself "this will be good for me." I am now a firm believer that every experience, the good and the bad, is an opportunity to learn and grow. By thinking this way, I in turn attract lessons and wisdom, and the universe responds. In learning this lesson, you too can become the author of your own experience, the gardener of your life. You see, there are no "bad" experiences; there are only bad thoughts about them. Similarly, there are no "good" experienced either; there are only good thoughts about them. When you act as if your experience is created from the outside in, you forfeit the power that is yours, and you play the role of a victim. The art of transcending the all too common way of seeing ourselves as a victim of whatever life throws our way, to seeing ourselves as the gardener of our life makes all the difference. With this one change, you change seats from being a back seat passenger, to being the driver, with all the controls within your reach.

Ask and You Will Receive

The second lesson this experience in Florida taught me was to ASK! Ironically, this idea was not foreign to me at all. As a former pastor, I used to teach and practice this idea daily. But when I left the church, I apparently left some valuable lessons as well. Thankfully, the universe re-introduced this lesson to me again. Since then, I make it a habit of asking. And I ask for big things. I realized that if I ask for small things, I get small responses. When I ask for big things, I get big responses. I don't always get exactly what I asked for, in exactly the form or shape I asked for it. But when I ask, I always receive. Without exception, every instance where

I've asked for a raise since then, I've received one. The last time I asked for a raise, I asked for a 10% raise without putting much thought into it. The more I considered my request, the more I regretted not asking for more. So, I went back and asked for a 79% raise instead of just a 10% raise. Did I get a 79% raise? Nope. Ha! But, I did receive a 16% raise instead of just the 10% raise I had initially asked for.

Whether asking for a raise, a personal request in prayer, or a favor from a friend, the principle is the same - if you ask with confidence, believe that you will receive, and *you will*. And if you don't ask, more times than not, you will not receive. It's really just that simple.

Jessie B. Rittenhouse captures this universal truth in the poem "My Wage":

I bargained with Life for a penny,
And Life would pay no more,
However I begged at evening
When I counted my scanty store;

For Life is just an employer,
He gives you what you ask,
But once you have set the wages,
Why, you must bear the task.

I worked for a menial's hire,
Only to learn, dismayed,
That any wage I had asked of Life,
Life would have paid.

With those lessons in mind, take some time every day to imagine. Dream bigger. Envision what your life would be like if these dreams came true. Imagine how it would change your career. Imagine how it would shape your relationships. Dream of what your daily life would look like if you were living your dreams. As you dream, just like in brainstorming, don't discredit any ideas that come to mind. Believe that anything and everything is possible. This practice of seeing your dreams is the first step to living them. Having a vision creates within you a desire to have what you dream of. Seeing in your mind the positive effects that would come about because of your dreams fruition ignites a blazing belief in the possibilities. What was once just a pipe dream becomes more of a goal to lay plans to. The more you imagine, the more your dreams turn into real things; things you can see, and things you can work toward achieving. So, dream big! Every great leader was a dreamer before they were a doer. Later in this book I will share some practical strategies for being the do-er, but you can't bypass the birthplace of your dreams (that is your imagination). And remember as you dream, our only limitations are the ones we create in our own minds.

DREAM BLOCKERS: *Choosing to view circumstances in negative light, playing the role of helpless victim to your circumstances, not asking for what you want or need*

SEEDS TO YOUR DREAMS: *View every experience as a gift from life to help you learn and grow, take responsibility for the life you live, ask for not only your needs but your wants*

CHAPTER 8

Believing Your Dreams

"Faith is the element of thought that transforms the ordinary vibration of thought into a spiritual vibration. "

-Napoleon Hill

Disbelief pushes what you want away, but belief draws it in like a magnet. In his landmark bestseller *Think and Grow Rich*, Napoleon Hill correctly explains the depth of thought which tends to go unconsidered by most: "...our brains become magnetized with the dominating thoughts we hold in our minds. These 'magnets' attract to us the forces, the people, the circumstances of life which *harmonize* with the nature of our dominating thoughts." The emotion behind belief (faith in our thoughts) carries an energy that says "yes" to the assistance of the universe in accomplishing your dreams. It's important to develop a genuine belief that the universe intends to support you. A favorite affirmation I learned from Louise Hay is "Life loves you and supports you in every possible way." It's important that you realize that your thoughts and beliefs carry energy. Everything does. The music you choose to listen to has energy. The shows and movies you entertain yourself with carry energy with them. And your thoughts and beliefs also have energy. When I write, I have a soothing music channel on my iPad that I always listen to, because it supports my writing. That is why you'll find most music services have certain music channels for certain activities. They have a workout or cardio channel, a studying channel, etc. These channels are curated to support what you're doing. The secret behind this idea is the energy the music carries with it.

Not only does the universe support our positive thoughts and beliefs, it also takes note of the negative thoughts and beliefs, and sends energy to support those also. As Hill also made mention in his book, "this power makes no attempt to discriminate between destructive and constructive thoughts, that it will urge us to translate into physical reality thoughts of poverty just as quickly as it will influence us to act upon thoughts of riches." The responsibility to control our thoughts falls on us, not the universe or God. The beauty of free will allows you to chart the course of your life. I would like to propose a few ways you can instill positive, life-giving thoughts and beliefs that will lead you to living the life of your dreams.

Affirmations

The vocabulary.com dictionary defines affirmation as "a big fat YES; an assertion that something is true." When we say an affirmation to ourselves, we are asserting that what we're saying is true. We are choosing a specific belief, and inviting the universe to support that belief. As pointed out before, this works with positive and negative affirmations. The power behind affirmations doesn't filter for you which thoughts or beliefs are healthy or helpful to fulfilling your dreams.

Begin today filtering what you say to be true. This includes the self-talk (things you say in your mind, or say to yourself when you're alone), as well as the comments you make to friends. I notice that many people these days have developed a sense of humor with the basis being self-deprecation, in other words the act of constant belittling, undervaluing, or being overly critical of oneself. Though this may seem humorous in the moment, the universe is always listening to support you with influential energy. If you constantly say that you are lazy, for example, don't be surprised when you find yourself always lacking energy or motivation.

Instead of asserting to be true attributes of yourself that will hinder your dreams, begin to develop language that supports your highest self. Even if statements of your highest self aren't currently true, affirming to yourself and the world that they are attracts a positive energy to assist you in becoming those things in reality. I have included some of my favorite affirmations to get you started. I assert these statements to be true several times throughout my day. And day-by-day, they become more and more true.

- Life loves you and supports you in every possible way.
- I am worthy of success.
- I am a strong, energetic person who makes healthy choices in my life.
- I have great friends who love and support me.
- I am a divine conduit for transforming the quality of people's lives through my job.

- There is time and space for everything I want to do today.
- Life brings me only good experiences. I am open to new and wonderful changes.
- Water energizes me and flushes my body of junk. It is my favorite beverage.
- I get plenty of sleep every night.
- I think big, and then allow myself to accept even more.
- I attract healthy friends.

These are only a few of my favorites. I also invite you to visit my website FeelFreetoGrow.com where you can subscribe to my daily Growth Affirmations.

The single greatest strategy for happiness and contentment is our ability to choose one thought over another. Choose to believe those thoughts that will support your dreams, not those that will sabotage them. And as you do, the universe will support you.

Make-Believe

As children, everyone has played make-believe. As we get older, most people tend to stop playing this game though, consigning it to something only children do. But there is actually a powerful element to make-believe that can help you live the life of your dreams.

In *Think and Grow Rich*, the author tells a story of a man who determined to be a business partner with Thomas Edison. He traveled to Mr. Edison's office and told him of his desire. He initially started working for Mr. Edison, but that was not his desire; he intended to be in business *with* Mr. Edison, not working *for* him. He had nothing to accredit him being deserving of this level of success; he had no money, very little education, no influence. But he did have initiative, belief, and the determination to see his dream become reality. For 5 years, to everyone else, he appeared to be just another employee of Mr. Edison, but to Edwin Barnes he was the partner of Thomas Edison every minute of that time. Eventually, a business opportunity presented itself to Barnes, and he took the chance, and indeed became a business partner with Mr. Edison (and became incredibly rich at the same time). Barnes literally believed his way into the reality of his dreams.

I have several experiences I could share that could describe times I believed my dreams into reality, but my favorite is related to my weight loss journey. In 2011 I was 70+ pounds overweight and miserable. As I shared in chapter 1, one of my weaknesses during this time was Mayfield's Moose Tracks ice cream. I had read time and again that no workout routine could make up for an unhealthy diet. I knew I needed to break my relationship with ice cream, but how? My answer came in the form of an affirmation. I began to assert several times a day, especially when I craved unhealthy foods, that "food is fuel, not fun." Now, the truth is, I loved food. It was a lot of fun to me. But realizing this belief was sabotaging my dream of losing weight, I decided to change this belief. My new belief, that the purpose of eating was to provide fuel and energy for my body, supported my dream. I ended up losing over 50 pounds, and I am now healthier than I've ever been in my adult life.

It's likely as you first begin to read affirmations to yourself you will think they aren't "true" to you. Then make-believe until they are true! Repetition of these new beliefs will cause your thoughts to change, and harmonize with beliefs that support your life goals.

Accepting What Is

Choosing to accept *what is* is fundamental to attaining peace in your life. Things happen, and many times we don't get our way. This is just life. No one escapes this reality. Things break, plans are canceled, employment ends, relationships drift apart, illness happens, some people do mean things, just to name a few less than desirable situations. The best thing you can do to maintain peace in these storms is just to accept *what is*. You certainly don't have to; life is just so much easier if you do. Any other response to these situations is just you arguing with reality. What good does that do?

Consider, as an example, the loss of a job. If you are like most, you depend on the income from your job to live on. So naturally the loss of this job, and the income it provides, will be disappointing. But overly stressing about this does you no good. Allowing yourself to live in a constant pity-party won't improve the situation either. Thinking to yourself negative thoughts towards the person or company who let you go won't bring your job back. Worrying about how your bills will get paid won't cause the direct deposit to continue coming in either.

The best response is to first accept what has happened (it happened whether you accept it or not, so you might as well make peace with it sooner rather than later), and then consider how you can learn and grow from the situation. I am confident that every situation in life presents with it opportunities to *learn* and *grow*. This habit of turning "negative" situations into "positives" develops resilience: the ability to recover quickly from difficulties. This is key to living the life of your dreams. Unfortunate circumstances *will come*. The key is to not camp there. Keep going, and keep growing. I've never met a strong, successful person with an easy past. In fact, the turning point in most successful people's lives comes at the moment of crisis in their life...a failed relationship that gives opportunity for self discovery and growth, a lost job that gives opportunity to finally start that dream business, an illness that leads to a healthier lifestyle.

So, when difficult or even painful experiences come your way, catch your breath, find quiet solitude, focus inward, remember your dreams, and find a way to grow. Life loves you, and supports you in every possible way; *believe* it.

DREAM BLOCKERS: *Saying, agreeing with and believing lies and ideas that oppose you and your dreams, arguing with life by not accepting what is*

SEEDS TO YOUR DREAMS: *Mentally and verbally affirm your highest self and your dreams, daydream about the life you want to live until you develop feelings about your dreams, choose to accept reality as it comes to you*

CHAPTER 9

Living Your Dreams

"Every morning you have the same two choices: continue to sleep with your dreams or get up and do something that brings them into reality."

-Joshua Perez

Every person I've shared my full life story with has responded by saying, "Wow, you should write a book." And my response until now has always been, "I'm going to, one day." Not anymore. I am now living that dream!

One night I was talking to my friend Ryan about my book ideas for the future. I was really just on a rabbit trail in the conversation; brainstorming out loud. He and I were talking about the idea of me writing a book because we had just recently returned from a short trip to the beach, and a message in my fortune cookie one evening reminded me of my dream: "You have a charming way with words and should write a book."

Something about the flattery in that fortune cookie really caught my attention. I couldn't get it off my mind. And I knew why...because I have always believed with certainty that dream would come true. Why hadn't the dream already come true though? The answer is simple: I hadn't taken action to begin living that dream. *Yet*. Even though I realize about 4 million fortune cookies are generated in factories each day, I knew there was something deeper happening. I knew it was time to write a book. *Life was inviting me to step into my dreams, and I had to respond.*

The next day, after having this brainstorming conversation with my friend, I immediately got to work. I even boldly declared on social media that I was writing a book. I did some research to formulate a plan for completing my first book, wrote out a schedule of writing, and then announced to the world that it would be done in that timeframe. I know how well I work under pressure, so I decided to create the pressure myself. And in 7 weeks, this book was completed.

In this final chapter, I am going to share with you some strategies I've learned through the years to help me accomplish big dreams. It's time to stop running after your dreams, and start living them!

Focused Life Plan

I've learned the best way to accomplish my dreams is to have specific, measurable, achievable, realistic, time-based goals (SMART Goals). I'm sure many reading this have heard of smart goals, but if you were honest, you probably don't have any SMART Goals related to your dreams. Every client I've ever coached has *heard* of SMART Goals, but none of them currently *had any* when I asked them. Just like the healthy living principles I shared in chapter 1 of this book, this is a commonly known principle that is very uncommonly applied in life.

To help change this, I am going to share a free plan with you that will help you establish your own specific, achievable, realistic goals which you can measure over time. The template is included in the appendix of this book, and you can also download a PDF copy for free by visiting www.FeelFreetoGrow.com. If you put into good use this plan, I guarantee you will go from being merely a *dreamer*, to someone who *lives the life of your dreams.*

Components of the Focused Life Plan

Goals: We attract our dreams into our lives when we have measurable goals and scheduled action plans. We set measurable goals or objectives for each area of life to help us live out our dreams. The primary areas of life you should develop dream goals for are: **spirituality, relationships (including the one with yourself), career, service to others, finances, health and fitness, and rest and relaxation.** We need long-term goals (more than 10 years) and short-term goals (3 months to 3 years).

Action Plans: We need an action plan for each long-term and short-term goal (in each area of life). Our action plan is the series of small steps we do that help us fulfill our goals. Goals that do not have an action plan will not be fulfilled. Therefore taking time to write an action plan is essential.

Schedule: Our "life" is made up of our *time*. Therefore we must establish a schedule that is in support of our dreams. If you don't determine your schedule, I assure you someone or something else will. Make a schedule for each action plan to provide focus for your priorities. A schedule is a target to aim at, or a "road map" to help us keep on track. Don't feel pressured to make your schedule line up with the expectations of others or what society considers "normal." For example, I used to insist that I workout in the mornings because it is said to be better for you. But you know what? I am NOT naturally a morning person. I eventually accepted this and stopped fighting it.

In making a schedule, we must allow for emergencies and unexpected things. It's okay to give yourself some grace. Trust me, I do not keep my schedule 100%. And that's okay. Even keeping your schedule 80% of the time will produce HUGE rewards!

One last important key to the focused life plan is to come back to it regularly to remind yourself of your locals, your action plans, and your schedule. I personally review my focused life plan every six months. Like the rest of the world, I review my goals at the beginning of each calendar year, and then I do the same again in early July. This allows me to see the progress I've made, and it's a great opportunity to make revisions to my plans. As you grow and learn and achieve your goals, it's normal for your priorities to need adjustments. See the *Focused Life Plan* in the appendix or visit www.FeelFreetoGrow.com to download a free copy!

Be Thankful For Your Dreams

There's always *what happens*, and then *what you think* about what happens. Many people are living some of their dreams even now, and yet they are unhappy, ungrateful, and to hear them tell it, nothing good ever comes their way. If they only did an accurate inventory of their lives, they would realize they are experiencing some of the fortunes they once only wished for. As the old gospel song goes, "Count your blessings, name them one by one."

One of my clients who experienced tremendous amounts of growth in his life while working with me once commented, "I always try to do good, but I feel like it never comes back to me." The truth is, this is just a mindset. You always reap what you sow. I encouraged him to intentionally begin looking for, and make a list of the good things that came his way over the next week. The following week, as soon as I brought that challenge up to him, he began to smile as he conceded that, sure enough, he was being showered with good things in his life.

So, as you begin to take these bold steps towards living your dreams, be sure to keep your eyes open to the possibility of actually seeing them come true. And when they do, don't forget the days when they were but a thought; a wish; a prayer. Don't forget how much they meant to you. Treasure them, and be thankful. I've noticed that the act of simply being thankful for the good in my life has attracted even more good to me. In fact, expressing gratitude is synonymous with saying, "I have received", and so I make a habit of thanking the universe for the good I believe is on the way to me already!

In the preceding chapters, I've shared with you foundational life strategies that, *if applied*, will cultivate a life where dreams come true. It's my great hope that you will allow this book to be a seed planted in your life for good things to come.

DREAM BLOCKERS: *Not having any goals or dreams, having no measurable actions you plan to take to move towards your dreams, not following any sort of plan or schedule in your life, not being thankful once your dreams enter your life*

SEEDS TO YOUR DREAMS: *Take the time to write out your goals, develop action plans and a schedule to work towards your goals, review and revise your goals and plans as you grow, be abundantly thankful each time one of your dreams come true*

Appendix

DOWNLOAD A FREE TEMPLATE OF
THE *FOCUSED LIFE PLAN* AT
WWW.FEELFREETOGROW.COM

Step One: Write out your dreams.

_____

_____

_____

_____

_____

_____

_____

_____

_____

_____

_____

_____

_____

_____

_____

_____

_____

_____

_____

_____

Step Two: Write out specific short-term (3 months to 3 years) & long-term (over 10 years) goals.

Spirituality
Short-term goals:

_____

_____

_____

Long-term goals:

_____

_____

_____

Relationships
Short-term goals:

_____

_____

_____

Long-term goals:

_____

_____

_____

Career

Short-term goals:

_____

_____

_____

Long-term goals:

_____

_____

_____

Service to Others

Short-term goals:

_____

_____

_____

Long-term goals:

_____

_____

_____

Finances

Short-term goals:

_____

_____

_____

Long-term goals:

_____

_____

_____

Health and Fitness

Short-term goals:

_____

_____

_____

Long-term goals:

_____

_____

_____

Rest and Relaxation

Short-term goals:

_____

_____

_____

Long-term goals:

_____

_____

_____

Step Three: Describe the specific things you will do to accomplish these goals.

Spirituality

Action Plan:

_____

_____

_____

_____

_____

_____

_____

Relationships

Action Plan:

_____

_____

_____

_____

_____

_____

Career

Action Plan:

_____

_____

_____

_____

_____

_____

Service to Others

Action Plan:

_____

_____

_____

_____

_____

_____

_____

Finances

Action Plan:

_____

_____

_____

_____

_____

_____

_____

Health and Fitness

Action Plan:

_____

_____

_____

_____

_____

_____

_____

Rest and Relaxation

Action Plan:

_____

_____

_____

_____

_____

_____

_____

Step Four: Schedule specific times you plan to take these actions. Some actions will be daily, and some will be weekly, monthly or annually.

Feel Free to Grow

Joshua Perez

Made in the USA
Columbia, SC
28 July 2024